21st Century Junior Library

Compsognathus

by Jennifer Zeiger

CHERRY LAKE PUBLISHING * ANN ARBOR, MICHIGAN

CHERRY
LAKE
Publishing

Published in the United States of America by Cherry Lake Publishing
Ann Arbor, Michigan
www.cherrylakepublishing.com

Content Adviser: Gregory M. Erickson, PhD, Dinosaur Paleontologist, Department of
Biological Science, Florida State University, Tallahassee, Florida

Reading Adviser: Marla Conn, Read with Me Now

Photo Credits: Cover, ©Stocktrek Images, Inc./Alamy; pages 4, 6, 8, 10, and 18, ©Linda Bucklin/
Shutterstock, Inc.; page 12, ©STT0008142/Media Bakery; page 14, ©STT0007399/
Media Bakery; page 16, ©STT0007398/Media Bakery; page 20, ©ASSOCIATED PRESS

LIBRARY OF CONGRESS CATALOGING-IN-PUBLICATION DATA
Zeiger, Jennifer.
  Compsognathus/by Jennifer Zeiger.
     p. cm.—(21st century junior library) (Dinosaurs)
  Includes bibliographical references and index.
  ISBN 978-1-61080-462-2 (lib. bdg.)—ISBN 978-1-61080-549-0 (e-book)—
ISBN 978-1-61080-636-7 (pbk.)
  1. Compsognathus—Juvenile literature. I. Title.
  QE862.S3Z45 2013
  567.912—dc23   2012001732

*Cherry Lake Publishing would like to acknowledge the work of
The Partnership for 21st Century Skills.
Please visit www.21stcenturyskills.org for more information.*

Printed in the United States of America
Corporate Graphics Inc.
July 2012
CLFA11

CONTENTS

Compsognathus was small but fast.

Tiny Dino

It is a warm, sunny afternoon. A giant **dinosaur** reaches its long neck into a tree to eat leaves. Another large dinosaur with big, sharp teeth sniffs the air. Far below them is a smaller dinosaur. It darts after a lizard on the ground. This little dinosaur is known as the *Compsognathus*.

The *Compsognathus* was tiny compared to other dinosaurs, including the *Giganotosaurus*.

The *Compsognathus* lived about 150 million years ago in what is now Europe. It was one of the smallest dinosaurs in history. The *Compsognathus* was only a little bigger than a chicken. Other dinosaurs alive at this time were as big as six elephants!

Think!

Most dinosaurs were much larger than the *Compsognathus*. How do you think the *Compsognathus*'s small size helped it? How did its size hurt it? Why do you think other dinosaurs were so big?

This dinosaur's strong legs helped it
outrun other dinosaurs.

Built to Run

The *Compsognathus* stood on two legs. Its arms were very small, but its legs were long and very strong. They helped it run fast. The *Compsognathus* could run fast enough to catch a speedy lizard.

The *Compsognathus* weighed about the same as a house cat.

Birds have **hollow** bones. This makes them lightweight so they can fly. The *Compsognathus* also had hollow bones. It did not weigh much. But the *Compsognathus* did not fly. Instead, its hollow bones helped it run very fast without using much energy.

Balance allowed the *Compsognathus* to run fast and make quick turns.

The *Compsognathus* had a long tail. The tail helped it stay **balanced**. Balance allowed it to run and turn without falling.

The *Compsognathus* also had a long neck. The neck could bend easily. This helped the *Compsognathus* look around without turning its body.

Create!

Draw a picture of a *Compsognathus* on a piece of paper. Label its legs, arms, tail, and neck. Try to label parts of the body you haven't read about yet, too. How did each part help the dinosaur survive?

Scientists know the *Compsognathus* ate lizards.
They know this because the bones of a lizard were
found in a *Compsognathus*'s stomach.

Chasing Down Dinner

A **carnivore** is an animal that eats meat. The *Compsognathus* was a carnivore. Scientists believe it ate lizards, bugs, and fish. It also ate small **mammals** similar to mice and rats. It used its speed and balance to catch them.

The *Compsognathus's* name means "dainty jaw." It was named this because of its tiny, sharp teeth.

The *Compsognathus* had a long,
slender head. Each of its two eyes was on
either side of its head. These eyes were big.
They gave the *Compsognathus* sharp vision.

Look!

Take a look at a picture of a **Compsognathus**. Check out its teeth and claws. Do they look scary? Would you want to run into a living **Compsognathus**? Does its small size change how dangerous it would be?

The *Compsognathus* had an small extra claw above its ankle. This claw is called a dewclaw.

Each finger on the *Compsognathus*'s hands had a sharp claw. The *Compsognathus* used these claws to grab **prey** and pick them up. It also used sharp toe claws to pin prey to the ground. The *Compsognathus* could also pick up prey with its sharp teeth.

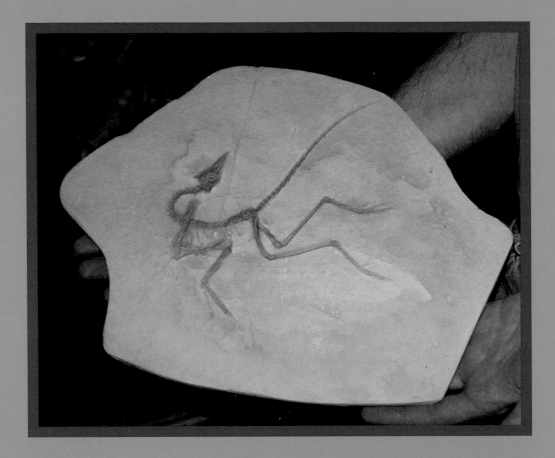

Scientists learn more each time another *Compsognathus* fossil is found.

Animal of the Past

There are no *Compsognathus* living today. Scientists study them by looking at **fossils**. They are still learning about the *Compsognathus*. Did it have feathers? Was it a good swimmer? Maybe one day you will be the scientist who discovers the truth!

GLOSSARY

balanced (BAL-unsd) steady, able to stay up without falling

carnivore (KAHR-nuh-vor) an animal that eats meat

dinosaur (DYE-nuh-sor) a kind of large reptile that lived millions of years ago

fossils (FAH-suhlz) the preserved remains of living things from thousands or millions of years ago

hollow (HAH-loh) empty inside

mammals (MAM-uhlz) one kind of animal that has fur and usually gives birth to live babies

prey (PRAY) an animal that is hunted by other animals for food

slender (SLEN-dur) thin

FIND OUT MORE

BOOKS

Bingham, Caroline. *DK First Dinosaur Encyclopedia*. New York. DK Publishing, 2007.

Gray, Susan H. *Compsognathus*. Chanhassen, MN: The Child's World, 2010.

WEB SITES

Enchanted Learning— Compsognathus
www.enchantedlearning.com/ subjects/dinosaurs/dinos/ Compy.shtml
Read all about the *Compsognathus* and print out a coloring page of the dino.

KidsDinos.com— Compsognathus
www.kidsdinos.com/ dinosaurs-for-children. php?dinosaur=Compsognathus
Learn more about the *Compsognathus* and follow links to learn about lots of other dinosaurs.

INDEX

ABOUT THE AUTHOR

Jennifer Zeiger graduated from DePaul University. She now lives in Chicago, Illinois, where she writes and edits books for children.